EP Language Arts 3
Workbook

This book belongs to:

_____

EP Language Arts 3 Workbook

ISBN-13: 978-1545251621
ISBN-10: 1545251622

First Edition: May, 2017

About this Workbook

This is an offline workbook for Easy Peasy All-in-One Homeschool's Language Arts 3 course. We've modified and expanded upon the online activities and printable worksheets available at the Easy Peasy All-in-One Homeschool website (www.allinonehomeschool.com) so that your child can work offline if desired. Whether you use the online or offline versions, or a combination of both, your child will enjoy these supplements to the Easy Peasy Language Arts course.

How to use this Workbook

This workbook is designed to be used in conjunction with Easy Peasy's Language Arts 3 Parent's Guide. As you proceed through the Parent's Guide, use this workbook to exercise your child's language arts skills.

This workbook follows the EP online Language Arts course in sequential order, providing 180 daily activity worksheets which can replace online activities and printable worksheets. The daily worksheets are designed with the following guidelines in mind:

- **To supplement daily lessons**

  This workbook on its own supplements, but does not replace, EP's daily lessons. Be sure to check the daily lesson on the website or in the Parent's Guide before having your child do the workbook activities.

- **To serve as an alternative to online activities**

  This workbook serves as an alternative to the activities posted online, providing offline activities in sufficient quantities and varieties to challenge your child. When used in conjunction with the Parent's Guide, this workbook becomes a complete offline course.

Please note, in the various places where nouns, verbs, and adjectives are practiced, certain words can be categorized in more than one place (you can go for a swim [noun] or you can swim [verb]). If your child marks one of them differently than the answer key indicates, have a conversation with them to find out why.

Available Online

- The printable worksheets, a subset of this workbook, are available online.
- The solutions are on the website as well as in the Parent's Guide and are **not included** in this workbook.

Completion Chart for Lessons 1 - 45

#		#		#	
1	my information	16	writing/spelling	31	spelling
2	copywork	17	writing	32	writing
3	copywork	18	writing	33	writing
4	copywork	19	writing	34	writing
5	I love you poem	20	writing	35	nouns
6	spelling	21	spelling	36	spelling
7	rhyming/alliteration	22	copywork	37	writing/capitalization
8	write a poem	23	alphabetical order	38	grammar review
9	acrostic poem	24	writing	39	writing
10	theme poem	25	writing/alphabetical order	40	capitalization/ punctuation
11	writing/spelling	26	spelling	41	spelling
12	writing	27	writing	42	writing/punctuation/ capitalization
13	writing	28	alphabetical order	43	capitalization/ punctuation
14	writing	29	capitalization/ punctuation	44	writing
15	writing	30	writing	45	copywork

Completion Chart for Lessons 46 - 90

#		#		#	
46	spelling	61	spelling	76	spelling
47	friendly letter	62	writing	77	writing
48	proofreading	63	noun and verb review	78	adjectives
49	writing	64	writing	79	writing
50	prefixes/suffixes	65	punctuation	80	correct the sentences
51	prefixes	66	spelling	81	spelling
52	writing	67	conjunctions	82	writing
53	capitalization/ punctuation	68	helping verbs	83	adjectives and antonyms
54	writing	69	conjunctions	84	writing
55	quotation marks	70	main and helping verbs	85	contractions
56	syllables	71	spelling	86	spelling
57	writing/quotation marks	72	writing	87	writing
58	contractions	73	adjectives	88	adjectives and synonyms
59	writing	74	writing	89	writing
60	writing	75	proofreading	90	compound words

Completion Chart for Lessons 91-135

91	spelling	106	spelling	121	comparative adjectives
92	writing	107	story summary	122	homophones/ homonyms
93	describe with adjectives	108	story summary	123	comparative or superlative
94	writing	109	story summary	124	main idea
95	writing	110	story summary	125	writing
96	spelling	111	spelling	126	superlative adjectives
97	short story	112	spelling	127	paragraph writing
98	adjectives and nouns	113	writing	128	comparative or superlative
99	short story	114	main idea and details	129	paragraph writing
100	writing	115	verbs	130	verbs
101	spelling	116	spelling	131	writing
102	summary	117	main idea and details	132	writing
103	adjectives and nouns	118	adjectives and nouns	133	writing
104	writing	119	writing	134	paragraph writing
105	prefixes and suffixes	120	verbs	135	verbs

Completion Chart for Lessons 136-180

#	Topic	#	Topic	#	Topic
136	spelling	151	plurals	166	spelling
137	writing	152	writing	167	final project
138	main idea	153	parts of speech	168	final project
139	writing	154	writing	169	final project
140	vowel pairing	155	verbs	170	final project
141	spelling	156	plurals	171	final project
142	simple, compound, complex	157	writing	172	final project
143	simple, compound, complex	158	parts of speech	173	final project
144	writing	159	spelling	174	final project
145	writing	160	homophones	175	final project
146	plurals	161	plurals	176	final project
147	conjunctions	162	A Caterpillar's Voice	177	final project
148	conjunctions/compound sent.	163	parts of speech	178	final project
149	conjunctions/compound sent.	164	writing	179	final project
150	conjunctions/compound sent.	165	writing	180	final project

My Information

Using the lines below, print your full name, phone number, and address. Write carefully and neatly. *(NOTE: the teaching lesson for this and every worksheet is located in the Parent's Guide. That separate book is necessary to make the course complete.)*

Full name:

_____

Phone number:

_____

Address:

_____

_____

_____

Copywork

Copy at least three lines of poetry that are repeated in *The Lamb*, by William Blake. Write carefully and neatly.

Little lamb, who made thee?
Dost thou know who made thee,
Gave thee life, and bid thee feed
By the stream and o'er the mead;
Gave thee clothing of delight,
Softest clothing, woolly, bright;
Gave thee such a tender voice,
Making all the vales rejoice?
Little lamb, who made thee?
Dost thou know who made thee?

Little lamb, I'll tell thee;
Little lamb, I'll tell thee:
He is called by thy name,
For He calls Himself a Lamb.
He is meek, and He is mild,
He became a little child.
I a child, and thou a lamb,
We are called by His name.
Little lamb, God bless thee!
Little lamb, God bless thee!

_____

_____

_____

_____

_____

Copywork

Copy these portions of the first three stanzas from the poems *Laughing Song* and *A Cradle Song* by William Blake.

When the green woods laugh
When the meadows laugh
When the painted birds laugh

Sweet dreams
Sweet Sleep
Sweet smiles

_____

_____

_____

_____

_____

Copywork

Copy this second stanza from *Spring* by William Blake. Make it look like the poem.
Make sure you copy all of the punctuation and write it on nine lines.

Little boy,
Full of joy;
Little girl,
Sweet and small;
Cock does crow,
So do you;
Merry voice,
Infant noise;
Merrily, merrily to welcome in the year.

_____

_____

_____

_____

_____

_____

_____

I Love You Poem

Write an "I love you" poem to someone. Write at least three lines, but write more if you want to. You could write it with repeating words like this:

- I love you because…
- I love you because…
- I love you because…

_____

_____

_____

_____

_____

_____

_____

_____

Spelling

Use the words in the box to fill in the blanks. Use each word only once.

Short a/e words		Other words		Verb spotlight
every	grand	forms	iron	solve
west	stand	near	science	solved
vest	batteries	high	school	solving
				solves

Put the <u>short a/e words</u> in alphabetical order.

_____   _____   _____

_____   _____   _____

Which of the <u>other words</u> have more than one syllable?

_____   _____

Which word is a **synonym** for *nigh*?   Which word is an **antonym** for *low*?

_____   _____

Which <u>other word</u> is plural?

_____

Write the remaining <u>other word</u>.

_____

Use a <u>verb spotlight</u> verb in a sentence that ends in a question mark.

_____

_____

Rhyming and Alliteration

Make a list of five pairs of rhyming words. Example: sweet feet.

_____

_____

_____

_____

_____

Now make a list of five pairs of words that start with the same sound (**alliteration**). Examples: tell time, pickled pepper, nosy neighbor.

_____

_____

_____

_____

_____

Write a Poem

Write a poem with the same rhythm as *The Fly* by William Blake. The first line has three syllables. The other three lines have four syllables. Example:

> *My big toe*
> *Has got an itch*
> *I'd buy a scratch*
> *If I were rich*

You don't have to rhyme the second and fourth lines, but if you do, get a high five and/or hug.

_____

_____

_____

_____

The Fly

Little Fly,
Thy summer's play
My thoughtless hand
Has brushed away.

Am not I
A fly like thee?
Or art not thou
A man like me?

For I dance,
And drink, and sing,
Till some blind hand
Shall brush my wing.

If thought is life
And strength and breath,
And the want
Of thought is death;

Then am I
A happy fly.
If I live,
Or if I die.

Acrostic Poem

Write a poem about this month. Whatever month it is, write that down the lines, one letter on each line. Then write one word on each line that starts with the letter listed. This is called an **acrostic** poem. For instance, if it were February you might write:

Freezing
Energy
Birthday…
etc.

_____

_____

_____

_____

_____

_____

_____

_____

Theme Poem

Write a poem about an apple. When you're finished, your apple poem will be in the shape of an apple.

Writing

Use these lines to write your poem.

_____

_____

Spelling

Use the words in the box to fill in the blanks. Use each word only once.

Short i/o/u words		Other words		Verb spotlight
slip	clog	between	motion	thump
inches	lunch	country	yard	thumped
pond	hug	plant	waves	thumping
				thumps

Put the short i/o/u words in alphabetical order.

_____   _____   _____

_____   _____   _____

Which of the other words have more than one syllable?

_____   _____   _____

Which other word is plural?   Write the remaining two other words.

_____   _____   _____

Use a verb spotlight verb in a sentence that ends in an exclamation point.

_____

_____

Writing

Write a poem about the month it is right now. Draw a picture in the box.

_____

_____

_____

_____

_____

_____

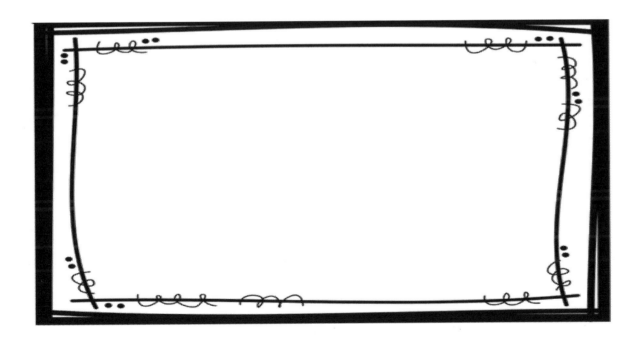

Writing

Write a poem about a sunset.

_____

_____

_____

_____

_____

_____

_____

Writing

Write two lines of poetry that rhyme. Try to make each line 8 syllables. You can draw a picture if you'd like.

_____

_____

_____

_____

_____

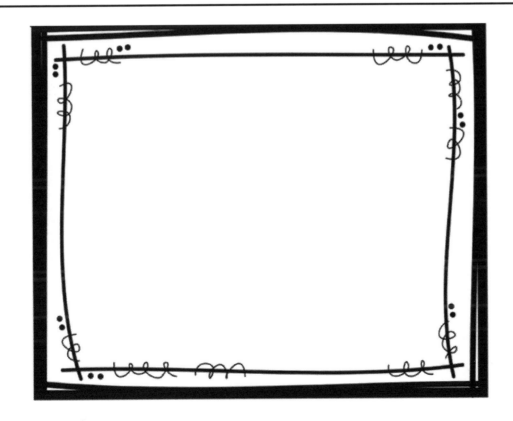

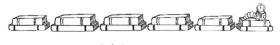

Writing

Write a poem about something sweet! Use the words in the box to create your poem.

fragrant	chewy	syrupy	delicious	sugary
swirly	crunchy	scrumptious	sticky	rippled
fudge	candy	toffee	ice cream	cake	pie
up	down	as	though	to	yet	is	not
was	what	over	the	above	beneath	in
but	always	so	and	with	at	under	on

_____

_____

_____

_____

_____

    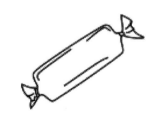

Writing

Write a color poem. Choose a color and write at least five lines.

_____

_____

_____

_____

_____

Spelling

Use the words in the box to fill in the blanks. Use each word only once.

Long a/long e words		Other words		Verb spotlight
save	easy	dresses	value	scream
sail	keep	father	area	screamed
grade	theme	pool	matter	screaming

Which of the words outside of the <u>verb spotlight</u> have more than one syllable?

_____   _____   _____

_____   _____   _____

Which of the remaining <u>long a/long e words</u> end with a silent e?

_____   _____   _____

Copy the <u>long a/e words</u> and the <u>other word</u> with a vowel pair in the middle.

_____   _____   _____

Write a sentence using a <u>verb spotlight</u> word.

_____

Writing

Write a bio poem, a poem about yourself. Follow the directions for each line.

Line 1: Write your first name.
Line 2: Write 3 adjectives that describe you.
Line 3: Write 3 things you love.
Line 4: Write your favorite food.
Line 5: Write an accomplishment.
Line 6: Write something you want to experience.
Line 7: Write your last name.

_____

_____

_____

_____

_____

_____

_____

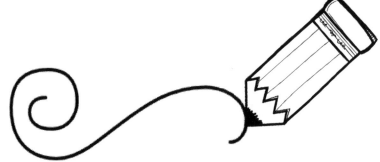

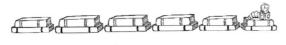

Writing

Write a list poem. You can use the beginning below if you can't think of your own.
Here is an example:

Beginning: I needed to get out of bed
But this is what I did instead:

List: *I laid around and played some games,*
I wrote a list of baby names,
I watched a movie on TV,
I drew a picture on my knee,
I dreamed I was a kangaroo
Who entertained folks at the zoo.
When I woke up I read a book
On how to sew and bake and cook.

_____

_____

_____

_____

_____

_____

_____

Writing

Write a theme poem about a flower in the shape of this flower. You can color it if you'd like.

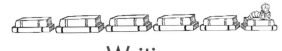
Writing

Write any poem you'd like today. Draw a picture that goes with your poem in the frame at the bottom.

_____

_____

_____

_____

_____

_____

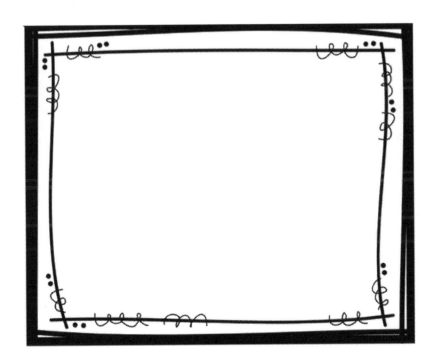

Spelling

Use the words in the box to fill in the blanks. Each word is only used once.

Long i/long o words		Other words		Verb spotlight
sign	hope	trade	current	check
tiny	stone	start	else	checked
wife	stole	earth	raise	checking
				checks

Put the <u>long i/long o words</u> in alphabetical order.

_____   _____   _____

_____   _____   _____

Which of the <u>other words</u> have a sound similar to the end of *together*?

_____   _____

Which word is a **synonym** for *begin*?   Which word is an **antonym** for *lower*?

_____   _____

Which remaining <u>other word</u> has a silent e to make a long vowel sound?

_____

Write the remaining <u>other word</u>.

_____

Choose a word from the <u>verb spotlight</u> and use it in a sentence that ends in an exclamation point.

_____

_____

Copywork

Copy four morals from this list compiled from *Aesop's Fables*. Make sure that you copy carefully to practice spelling and punctuation.

A man is known by the company he keeps.
Acquaintance softens prejudices.
Avoid even appearances of danger.
Birds of a feather flock together.
Misfortune tests the sincerity of friends.
Necessity is the mother of invention.
Pride goes before destruction.

Like will draw like.
Attempt not impossibilities.
Beware of unequal matches.
Distance exaggerates dangers.
Might makes right.
Nip evil in the bud.
The memory of a good deed lives.

Alphabetical Order

Put each row of words in alphabetical order by numbering the lines beside them. Sing the ABC song to yourself if you need help!

_____ bear   _____ dog   _____ cat   _____ fox

_____ half   _____ third   _____ fourth   _____ sixth

_____ peach   _____ cherry   _____ apple   _____ banana

 van   _____ train     boat   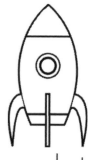 rocket

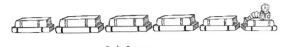

Writing

Write a story that would teach this lesson: *look before you leap*. If you need help, here's a starter idea (you can feel free to come up with your own): *Peter's friend Ryan ran up to him and asked if he wanted to go pernickle picking. Peter didn't want Ryan to know he didn't know what pernickles were, so he said yes and went along. (Pernickle is a made up thing. What would happen next to teach the lesson, look before you leap?)*

_____

_____

_____

_____

_____

_____

_____

Writing

Write a **moral** or a lesson. What should people know? For examples of morals, you can look at the list on lesson 22.

_____

_____

_____

Alphabetical Order

Put each row of words in alphabetical order by numbering the lines beside them. Sing the ABC song to yourself if you need help!

____baby   ____penguin   ____carrot   ____feet

____shoe   ____tree   ____cup   ____muffin

Spelling

Use the words in the box to fill in the blanks. Use each word only once.

st/str blend words		Other words		Verb spotlight
strong	least	upon	base	reach
strip	burst	next	expand	reached
stream	east	own	calculate	reaching
				reaches

Which of the <u>other words</u> have more than one syllable?

_____   _____   _____

Which of the <u>blend words</u> have three consonants in a row?

_____   _____   _____

_____

Which of the remaining words start with a vowel?

_____   _____

Put the remaining words outside of the <u>verb spotlight</u> in alphabetical order.

_____   _____   _____

Use one <u>verb spotlight</u> verb in a sentence that ends in a period and another in a sentence that ends in a question mark.

_____

_____

_____

_____

Writing

Write three questions. They should be questions you want answered. Ask someone or find the answers some other way.

1 _____

_____

2 _____

_____

3 _____

_____

Alphabetical Order

Put each section of words in alphabetical order by numbering the lines beside them. If the first letters match, check the second letters. If the second letters match, check the third, and so on.

_____ caterpillar   _____ butterfly

_____ anteater   _____ elephant   _____ flamingo

_____ flower   _____ fish

_____ feet   _____ father   _____ fountain

_____ church   _____ chicken

_____ chair   _____ cheer   _____ chops

_____ string   _____ strawberry

_____ stroll   _____ strength   _____ struck

Capitalization

Underline the words that need to be capitalized. Remember that all sentences begin with a capital letter and proper nouns should be capitalized.

my doctor's name is bernadette wilson.

our family went to los angeles in february.

where is the nearest burger king?

uncle charlie and i are going to indiana on tuesday.

timothy winkle plays soccer at garfield park.

will you come with us to siam palace for dinner?

my dad will have knee surgery at central hospital.

abraham lincoln signed the emancipation proclamation.

who is hosting christmas dinner this year?

there's a potluck at calvary church on sunday.

jingle bells was really written for a thanksgiving program.

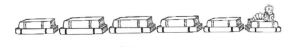

Writing

Write all of these words two times each. Make sure you spell them correctly:
knights, calendar, your, friend, their.

_____

_____

_____

_____

_____

Spelling

Use the words in the box to fill in the blanks. Use each word only once.

kn/wr words		Other words		Verb spotlight
known	wrong	while	sum	think
knock	wrist	product	digit	thought
knife	wrinkle	subtract	round	thinking
				thinks

Which of the <u>other words</u> are math words?

_____   _____   _____

_____   _____

Which of the remaining words have a silent e?

_____   _____   _____

Which word is a synonym for *incorrect*?   Which is an antonym for *unknown*?

_____   _____

The two remaining words both have a silent letter. Write the words here:

_____   _____

Use one <u>verb spotlight</u> verb in a sentence that includes a pronoun.

_____

_____

Writing

Copy this sentence: *As he's her grandfather, it is high time he should do something for the child.*

_____

_____

_____

_____

What is the contraction in the sentence?   What does it stand for?

_____   _____

Write another contraction here.   What does it stand for?

_____   _____

Comma Time

Fill in the missing commas in the lists below. Remember to add commas when you have three or more nouns, verbs, or adjectives in a row.

Is your favorite subject math science or history?

We went to the store the library and the bank yesterday.

Carrie Scott and Amanda went to the movie theater.

I love to run jump and play in the snow.

We have to shop eat and walk a lot in New York City.

My mom is smart beautiful kind and generous.

The tall quiet patient doctor answered my questions.

Every man woman and child deserves food shelter and love.

The goat the cow and the dog all watched as the short fluffy black sheep tried to find the flock.

Bonus:

Tim Jack and Bill scrimped saved and hoarded their pennies nickels and dimes.

Writing

Write a conversation you would have with your grandfather if it was the first time you met him. What would you want to ask him? What would you want to tell him? Write your conversation in a dialogue format like this:

me: Hi.

GF: Who do we have here? (GF stands for grandfather.)

_____

_____

_____

_____

_____

_____

Writing

Rewrite your conversation with your grandfather, this time using quotation marks and speech tags to show who said what, like this:

"Hi," I said.

"Who do we have here?" asked Grandfather.

_____

_____

_____

_____

_____

_____

Spelling

Use the words in the box to fill in the blanks. Use each word only once.

gh/ph words		Other words		Verb spotlight
bought	graph	along	lady	break
laughed	paragraph	close	seem	broke
enough	photograph	something	street	breaking
				breaks

Which of the words outside of the <u>verb spotlight</u> have more than one syllable?

_____ _____ _____

_____ _____ _____

Which of the <u>gh/ph words</u> are in the past tense?

_____ _____

Which word is a homophone for *seam*?   Which is an antonym for *open*?

_____   _____

Write the two remaining words that aren't in the <u>verb spotlight</u> list.

_____ _____

Use one <u>verb spotlight</u> verb in a question.

_____

_____

Writing

Copy these sentences. Make sure you copy them exactly. When you're finished writing them, double check that they are correct: *The strong wind nearly blew her from her seat, so she hurried with her meal, to be able to go inside and up to her bed. She slept in it as well as a prince on his royal couch.*

_____

_____

_____

_____

_____

Capitalization

Underline the words that need to be capitalized. Remember that all sentences begin with a capital letter and proper nouns should be capitalized.

my dad is the principal at wildwood elementary.

the louvre is a famous museum in paris, france.

my brother, joey, went to san antonio on saturday.

Grammar Review

For each group of sentences, color in the circle next to the sentence that is written correctly. Pay special attention to capitalization and punctuation.

○ the bear cub came out of its den.
○ The mother bear came out after it.
○ The two bears played in the sun
○ Then they left in search of some food?

○ Mrs. Scott works at Lincoln Park.
○ Mr. Scott works at central library.
○ The two meet for lunch at Taco bell.
○ they enjoy spending the hour together.

○ Where did you go? asked my mother.
○ "I went to the playground." I answered.
○ "I got permission from Dad," I assured her.
○ She noticed Dad's note on the table

○ I love to eat carrots, broccoli, and green beans, for dinner.
○ My sister prefers corn, cauliflower, and squash.
○ My Dad is more of a meat, and potatoes kind of guy.
○ my mom just wants anyone else to cook!

○ Sylvia gave a report on glaciers
○ she said that she had seen some on her trip.
○ The class asked where she went on her trip?
○ She told us she took a cruise to Alaska.

○ My dog charlie is a cute little guy.
○ He wags his tail whenever he sees me
○ Charlie's favorite toy is a blue tennis ball.
○ He loves to run jump and roll over.

Writing

Imagine you spent a day on the mountain. Describe your day. What did you see? What did you smell? What happened? When you are finished, read over what you wrote. Be sure your sentences have proper capitalization and punctuation. Fix any mistakes.

_____

_____

_____

_____

_____

_____

_____

Capitalization and Punctuation

Correct the sentences by underlining the words that should be capitalized and adding any missing punctuation.

We were in chicago on sunday monday and tuesday.

the three girls dresses all matched.

My father and i threw hit and kicked the ball in the yard.

she wore green to the saint patrick's day parade.

It is so hot in july that I prefer to just stay inside

what do you like to eat for thanksgiving

don't touch that

my scissors glue and paper are all over the table

When maria comes home we will go to café maurice.

Should we wait for emily carrie and zandra to arrive

The united states has a wide range of weather.

My uncles car is in the shop until friday.

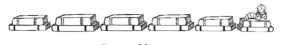

Spelling

Use the words in the box to fill in the blanks. Use each word only once.

ch/tch words		Other words		Verb spotlight
chance	match	front	difference	open
choose	batch	safe	property	opened
child	watch	whole	travel	opening
				opens

Put the <u>ch/tch words</u> in alphabetical order.

_____   _____   _____

_____   _____   _____

Which of the <u>other words</u> have three syllables?

_____   _____

Which word is a synonym for *journey*?   Which is an antonym for *back*?

_____   _____

Which of the <u>other words</u> have a silent e?

_____   _____

Use one <u>verb spotlight</u> verb in a command.

_____

_____

Writing

Copy these sentences carefully. Check your capitalization, punctuation, and spelling: *She had gone to the housekeeper and told her all about Heidi. The lady, delighted with the idea, had told her to fetch the child at once.*

_____

_____

_____

_____

_____

Capitalization and Punctuation

Correct the sentences by underlining the words that should be capitalized and adding any missing punctuation.

the ball top and jump rope were all in the toybox

the dogs name was max

seth and i went to southgate mall yesterday

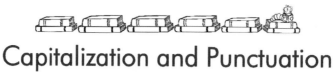

Capitalization and Punctuation

Correct the sentences by underlining the words that have capitalization errors and adding any missing punctuation. Use the clues to catch all of the mistakes.

These sentences each have 3 punctuation and 2 capitalization mistakes.

the boys Bathroom was a dirty disgusting stinky mess.

My mother said that carlas book was under janes car

Utah iowa and ohio are shorter state names

These sentences each have four total mistakes.

can you believe its snowing in october

main street is a block down from morton avenue.

My sisters favorite colors are pink purple and gold

Can you find all of the mistakes without any clues?

i cant believe it

where is the closest taco bell

football hockey and rugby are some dangerous sports

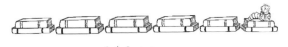

Writing

Write about a pretend day in a big city. When you're finished, read over what you wrote and fix any mistakes.

_____

_____

_____

_____

_____

_____

Copywork

Copy one of these quotations by Abraham Lincoln. Start like this: Abraham Lincoln said, "…" and put your quote (the words he said) between the quotation marks. Make sure you have a comma after *said*.

No man has a good enough memory to be a successful liar.
You cannot escape the responsibility of tomorrow by evading it today.
Whatever you are, be a good one.
Be sure you put your feet in the right place, then stand firm.
The best thing about the future is that it comes one day at a time.
When you reach the end of your rope, tie a knot and hang on.
The best way to destroy an enemy is to make him a friend.
If you look for the bad in people expecting to find it, you surely will.

_____

_____

_____

_____

_____

Spelling

Use the words in the box to fill in the blanks. Use each word only once.

Soft g words		Other words		Verb spotlight
giraffe	stage	paper	children	push
gentle	engine	mirror	ocean	pushed
ginger	badge	reflect	fraction	pushing
				pushes

Put the <u>other words</u> in alphabetical order.

_____   _____   _____

_____   _____   _____

Which <u>soft g words</u> have one syllable?

_____   _____

Which <u>soft g words</u> have a *short e* sound?

_____   _____

Which remaining <u>soft g word</u> has a silent e that does *not* make the vowel sound long?

_____

Write the remaining word from the <u>soft g words</u> list.

_____

Use a <u>verb spotlight</u> verb in a sentence that ends in an exclamation point.

_____

_____

Friendly Letter

Correct the friendly letter by choosing the proper correction for the bold portions.

HEADING - SALUTATION - BODY - CLOSING - SIGNATURE

November 30 2050
a. November 30, 2050
b. November, 30 2050
c. November 30 2050.
d. November 30, 2050.

Dear Mr Hinkle,
a. Dear Mr. Hinkle
b. Dear Mr Hinkle
c. Dear Mr. Hinkle,
d. Dear, Mr. Hinkle

Thank you for allowing me to come to your home for **thanksgiving** this year. I had a great time with your family.

a. thanksgiving,
b. Thanksgiving
c. Thanksgiving,
d. thanks giving

Do you have any plans for Christmas? I will be spending it with my grandparents in **Los angeles, C.A.**, this year. I don't think I will be seeing any snow!

a. los angeles, C.A.
b. Los Angeles C.A.
c. Los angeles, CA
d. Los Angeles, CA

I wish you a wonderful holiday season! Please tell your family that I said hello.

Yours Truly,
a. Yours truly,
b. Yours Truly
c. yours truly,
d. Yours truly:

Michael

Proofreading

Correct the sentences using the clues given. Underline the answer or write the correct word in the blank to fix the mistake.

Me and Samantha enjoy the library.
(Samantha and I/Samantha and me)

My mom am the driver that takes us there.
(are/is)

It is full of fun books for Samantha and I to take home.
(I and Samantha/Samantha and me)

We likes to look at the illustrations in the books.
(Make sure the verb matches the subject.)

_____

Yesterday we write our own stories.
(Make sure the tense matches throughout the sentence.)

_____

See if you can correct these sentences without any clues.

Does you have your own library card?

_____

What are your favorite kinds of book?

_____

Do you enjoy pictures like Samantha and I?

_____

Writing

Write a letter to your grandfather. If you're reading Heidi, you could write a letter home from Heidi to her grandfather. Use proper punctuation, capitalization, and spelling.

HEADING - SALUTATION - BODY - CLOSING - SIGNATURE

_____

_____

_____

_____

_____

_____

Prefixes and Suffixes

Match the prefix or suffix with the correct root word by underlining your choice.

mis_____   judge   yard   water   room

in_____   shirt   wall   side   color

dis_____   up   down   watch   appear

pre_____   bang   here   joke   flight

un_____   cape   tiny   cover   drink

il_____   floor   legal   skip   back

____able   chair   high   love   was

____ly   jump   quick   couch   bonus

____ing   stand   dog   over   pretty

____logy   shoe   brown   bio   hour

____er   car   flight   star   teach

____ness   check   bald   kiss   run

Prefixes

Read the definition. Then choose a prefix and root word that combine to match the definition. Write the complete new word in the blank.

Prefixes
un   mis   kilo   re   sub
anti   bi   over   under   tri

Root words
gram   marine   angle   cycle
cooked   happy   social
sleep   type   understand

Type again   _____

Sad   _____

Two wheels   _____

Three angles   _____

Under sea   _____

Not outgoing   _____

Not cooked enough   _____

Sleep too long   _____

Take in a wrong sense   _____

1000 grams   _____

Writing

Write a letter to your grandparents, a missionary, or anyone. Follow the techniques you've learned for writing a friendly letter. Read over your work when you are finished and correct any mistakes.

_____

_____

_____

_____

_____

_____

_____

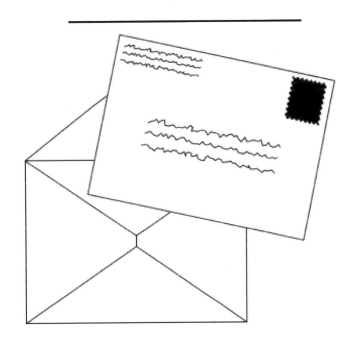

Capitalization and Punctuation

Correct the sentences by underlining the words that have capitalization errors and adding any missing punctuation. Use the clues to catch all of the mistakes.

These sentences each have 2 punctuation and 2 capitalization mistakes.

Uncle bills book was published on friday

Friday saturday and sunday are my favorite days.

why cant you come to portland with me

These sentences each have four total mistakes.

Im sorry youre so hot on this blistering august day

Where is central library in relationship to metro zoo?

my sisters name is carrie

Can you find all of the mistakes without any clues?

watch out for that hot stove

Can you please put away your jacket socks and shoes

My dads new drill will ship on tuesday.

Writing

Write a letter to the publisher of a book you recently read.

_____

_____

_____

_____

_____

_____

_____

_____

_____

_____

_____

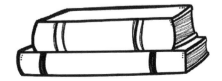

Quotation Marks

Add the missing punctuation to the sentences below by writing it in. Underline any words that should be capitalized that aren't.

Will you come with me to the store   asked Grandma

We need to get some bread and milk   she said

Then she added   I hope they aren't out of the things we need

Oh no! what will we do if they are   she worried

I said   calm down, Grandma. we will just try another store

Of course you're right, dear   she admitted

She continued sometimes I forget there are stores on every corner now

When I was a little girl we got everything from one general store. If they were out of what we needed we had to wait for them to order it she explained

I love your stories, Grandma. now let's go get that bread and milk. I'm ready for your famous French toast I exclaimed

Syllables

How many syllables are in the following words? Write the number of syllables in the blank beside the word. If you need help, put your hand under your chin and say the word out loud. The number of times your hand goes down is the number of syllables in the word.

caterpillar _____   bird _____

ladybug _____   apple _____

cupcake _____   bow _____

baseball _____   nest _____

butterfly _____   pencil _____

sailboat _____   carrot _____

balloon _____   basket _____

bicycle _____   egg _____

flower _____   cereal _____

baby _____   fox _____

Writing

Think of a friend or relative you could visit. Write a packing list. What would you need to bring (would it be cold or warm)? What would you bring as gifts? Write ten things on your list.

1. _____   2. _____

3. _____   4. _____

5. _____   6. _____

7. _____   8. _____

9. _____   10. _____

Quotation Marks

Add the missing punctuation to the sentences below by writing it in.

Will you please keep your voice down   asked the librarian

The doctor said   I need to look in your ears now

My sister screamed   Ahhhhh as she flew down the hill on her bike

Contractions

Write what each contraction means in the blank beside it. If you're stuck, try using the contraction in a sentence and figure out what it means that way.

aren't _____   you'd _____

can't _____   we'll _____

they've_____   it's _____

I'd _____   they're _____

haven't_____   I'm _____

won't _____   isn't _____

shouldn't_____   it'll _____

you're _____   we'd _____

she'll _____   wouldn't_____

you've _____   he'll _____

Writing

Write a short story describing what you would see if you were visiting someone in another country. If you can't decide on a country, choose Australia. You could start it like this: *While I was visiting my friend in Australia,*

_____

_____

_____

_____

_____

_____

_____

Writing

Write a dialogue between you and the friend you visited in another country from lesson 59. When the next person starts talking, start on a new line. Put everything that's said out loud in "quotation marks" like this:

"What's it like living in Australia?" I asked.

"It's definitely hot," answered Paul.

_____

_____

_____

_____

_____

Spelling

Use the words in the box to fill in the blanks. Use each word only once.

oi sound words		Other words		Verb spotlight
choice	royal	group	otter	walk
voice	annoy	oddly	forest	walked
noise	destroy	night	equation	walking
				walks

Which oi sound words have more than one syllable?

_____   _____   _____

Which oi sound words have a *silent e*?

_____   _____   _____

Which other words have a *short* o sound?

_____   _____

Which other words have a different o sound?

_____   _____

Which other word is an antonym for *day*?

_____

Which other word helps you solve a math problem?

_____

Use a verb spotlight verb in a sentence that contains a quotation.

_____

_____

Writing

Write a song.

_____

_____

_____

_____

_____

_____

_____

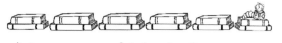

Noun and Verb Review

Review your nouns and verbs. Remember that nouns are people, places, things, and ideas. Verbs show action or a state of being.

Underline the nouns in the following sentences.

The game we played yesterday was fun.

The children are yelling loudly!

Our library is big and quiet.

Will your mother be back soon?

Underline the verbs showing action in the following sentences.

The game we played yesterday was fun.

The children are yelling loudly!

Underline the verbs showing a state of being in the following sentences.

Our library is big and quiet.

Will your mother be back soon?

Writing

Write a letter to your grandparents, a missionary, or anyone. Follow the techniques you've learned for writing a friendly letter. Read over your work when you are finished and correct any mistakes.

_____

_____

_____

_____

_____

_____

_____

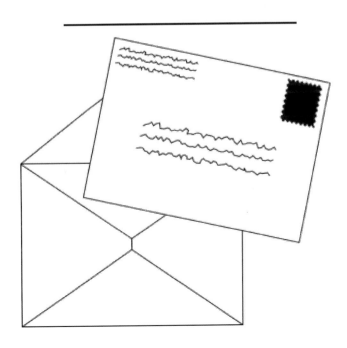

Punctuation

Fill in the missing punctuation from each of the sentences.

My sisters doll was left outside and it got wet muddy and gross.

The three boys shoes were stinky after a day of baseball.

My dad drove us to practice and said We need to clean out this van.

Have you ever been to Chicago Illinois

Her birthday is December 20 but she celebrates it in the fall when people arent so busy.

My dogs name is Max and her dogs names are Sparky Rover and Rex.

Watch out screamed my brother. Theres a snake in the yard

Spelling

Use the words in the box to fill in the blanks. Use each word only once.

ou sound words		Other words		Verb spotlight
shouted	crown	desert	began	take
around	growl	important	river	took
pounds	however	sea	influence	taking
				takes

Which <u>other words</u> have more than one syllable?

_____   _____   _____

_____   _____

Which <u>ou sound word</u> is past tense?   Which <u>ou sound word</u> is plural?

_____   _____

Which word is a synonym for ocean? Which <u>ou sound word</u> has three syllables?

_____   _____

Which remaining words outside of the <u>verb spotlight</u> have only one syllable?

_____   _____

Write the last word outside of the <u>verb spotlight</u>.

_____

Use a <u>verb spotlight</u> verb in a sentence that contains a list with commas.

_____

_____

Conjunctions

Write three sentences. The first needs to have **and**, the second **but**, and the third **or**. Write a sentence, a comma with your **conjunction**, and then another sentence.

Helping Verbs

Circle the letter next to the helping verb that correctly completes the sentence.

Amy, Laura, and I ___ going to the mall.

    a.   are

    b.   is

    c.   am

Laura ____ asking her mom to drive us.

    a.   are

    b.   is

    c.   am

We ____ look for new shoes for our dance class.

    a.   will

    b.   had

    c.   have

I ____ hoping to find some with sparkles and a strap.

    a.   are

    b.   is

    c.   am

We _____ enjoying our dance class this year.

    a.   have been

    b.   has been

    c.   will be

Conjunctions

Write three more sentences. The first needs to have **and**, the second **but**, and the third **or**. Write a sentence, a comma with your **conjunction** and then another sentence.

_____

_____

_____

_____

_____

_____

sentence   conjunction   sentence

Main Verbs and Helping Verbs

For each sentence, tell whether the underlined verb is a main verb or a helping verb by circling your answer.

We <u>are</u> going to dinner for my cousin's birthday.

main verb   helping verb

He is <u>turning</u> eight years old on Saturday.

main verb   helping verb

My cousin loves burgers, so I'm sure we <u>will</u> go to a burger place.

main verb   helping verb

He also <u>loves</u> superheroes and wears a cape everywhere he goes.

main verb   helping verb

I hope he <u>decides</u> not to wear it to the restaurant.

main verb   helping verb

We don't need anyone <u>tripping</u> over his cape while carrying food!

main verb   helping verb

I guess that <u>would</u> make for a memorable evening.

main verb   helping verb

I <u>love</u> my cousin despite his silly cape.

main verb   helping verb

Spelling

Use the words in the box to fill in the blanks. Use each word only once.

Short aw words		Other words		Verb spotlight
crawl	pause	sleep	once	carry
dawn	author	resemble	disappear	carried
paws	laundry	polygon	north	carrying
				carries

Put the other words in alphabetical order.

_____ _____ _____

_____ _____ _____

Which two short aw words are homophones of each other?

_____ _____

Which remaining short aw words only have one vowel?

_____ _____

Which short aw word is a synonym for writer?

_____

Write the last word that isn't a part of the verb spotlight.

_____

Use a verb spotlight verb in a sentence that ends with a question mark.

_____

_____

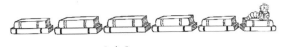

Writing

Pretend that you woke up today and all of the animals in the world could talk. Write a story about what animal/animals you talked to and what they said. Check for any mistakes when you are through. Be sure to use proper punctuation, including quotation marks.

_____

_____

_____

_____

_____

_____

Adjectives

Remember that an **adjective** is a word that describes a noun. Color in the adjective flowers below.

Writing

Write about your day as a _____. Choose something **inanimate** or not alive. Some ideas are a pencil, an umbrella, a spoon, a shoe, a computer... choose whatever you want!

_____

_____

_____

_____

_____

_____

Proofreading

Circle the letter of the option that best corrects the underlined portion of each sentence.

<u>bill said I</u> would love to go to the park with you tomorrow."

   a.   Bill said I

   b.   Bill said, "I

   c.   Bill said "I

Our library has books on <u>dragons knights and castles</u>.

   a.   dragons Knights and castles

   b.   dragons, knights, and, castles

   c.   dragons, knights, and castles

I <u>cant find my sisters</u> picture she made for our mom.

   a.   can't find my sister's

   b.   can't find my sisters'

   c.   can't find my sisters

Did you watch the news <u>Last Night.</u>

   a.   Last Night?

   b.   last night?

   c.   last night.

America's birthday is considered to be <u>July 4 1776</u>.

   a.   July 4, 1776

   b.   July, 4, 1776

   c.   July 4, 1776,

Spelling

Use the words in the box to fill in the blanks. Use each word only once.

long/short oo words		Other words		Verb spotlight
loose	shook	pentagon	shock	crash
balloon	looked	south	second	crashed
goose	understood	those	predict	crashing
				crashes

Which words outside of the <u>verb spotlight</u> have more than one syllable?

_____ _____ _____

_____ _____

Which words outside of the <u>verb spotlight</u> end in a *silent e*?

_____ _____ _____

Which word is a direction?

_____

Which remaining words start with the consonant blend *sh*?

_____ _____

Which remaining <u>long/short oo word</u> is past tense?

_____

Use a <u>verb spotlight</u> verb in a sentence that ends with an exclamation point.

_____

_____

Writing

Write a story about the time you were less than an inch tall. Use adjectives to describe what things looked like when you were teeny tiny. How did you get small? What did you do? What was it like?

_____

_____

_____

_____

_____

_____

_____

_____

_____

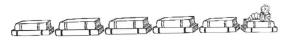
Adjectives

Underline the adjective that best completes the sentence. Both choices are adjectives, but which one better describes the noun?

The deck was _____ after the rain. (soaked/scratchy)

The phone was _____ with the ringer all the way up. (purple/loud)

Jane's _____ blue eyes sparkled as she smiled. (angry/beautiful)

It was _____ news that our lost dog had returned. (thrilling/tasty)

The _____ painting was hanging in a museum. (large/energetic)

Dinner last night was _____. (bright/delicious)

The _____ wind blew the trees as the storm raged. (harsh/fluffy)

The video game was _____. (brown/exciting)

Write in an adjective that fits with the sentence. Be as descriptive as you can.

The bird flew in a _____ line.

The gravel road felt really _____.

Our _____ driveway fits two cars.

The math whiz was incredibly _____.

Writing

Write about being in the woods. Write about all the things you see, hear, smell, feel, and taste. Read over your work when you are done and correct any mistakes.

_____

_____

_____

_____

_____

_____

_____

_____

Correct the Sentences

For each sentence, choose the sentence type by circling it. Then correct the first word and add proper punctuation.

show me how to build a snowman

statement   command   question   exclamation

where can I find some markers

statement   command   question   exclamation

i can't wait for summertime

statement   command   question   exclamation

i'm not sure where I left my book

statement   command   question   exclamation

my mom is really good at organizing things

statement   command   question   exclamation

please pick up your coat and hang it on the hook

statement   command   question   exclamation

the sun is shining brightly outside

statement   command   question   exclamation

what is your favorite season

statement   command   question   exclamation

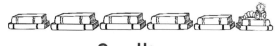

Spelling

Use the words in the box to fill in the blanks. Use each word only once.

air sound words		Other words		Verb spotlight
stairs	glare	almost	buy	miss
repair	compare	Indian	real	missed
airplane	prepare	among	quadrilateral	missing
				misses

Put the <u>air sound words</u> in alphabetical order.

_____   _____   _____

_____   _____   _____

Which <u>other word</u> is a proper noun?

_____

Which word is a synonym for *not quite*?   Which is an antonym for *fake*?

_____   _____

Which word has five syllables?   Which word can relate to money?

_____   _____

Write the remaining <u>other word</u>.

_____

Use a <u>verb spotlight</u> verb in a descriptive sentence with at least one adjective.

_____

_____

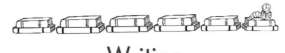

Writing

Write directions for how to do something. Make sure you include every step. Start with a sentence that tells what you are going to give instructions for. Then write your steps. Write words like *first, second, third, last* before each step. When you are done, ask someone to follow your instructions EXACTLY. Did they do it correctly, or did you miss something in your instructions?

_____

_____

_____

_____

_____

_____

Adjectives and Antonyms

Read each sentence and underline the adjective. Then rewrite the sentence using the antonym or opposite of the adjective from the word box. For example, if the original sentence was *The windows are not clean*, *clean* would be the adjective and *dirty* would be its antonym. Your new sentence would be *The windows are dirty*.

cold	loud	down	wet	fast	happy
long	hard	young	broken		

This book is not short.   _____

My brother is not quiet.   _____

Our radio is not functional. _____

That race was not slow.   _____

The girl is not sad.   _____

The man is not old.   _____

The air is not warm.   _____

The sun is not up.   _____

The concrete is not soft.   _____

The towel is not dry.   _____

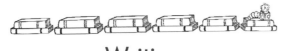

Writing

Write about something important you have learned. Tell how you learned it and why it has been an important lesson to you.

_____

_____

_____

_____

_____

_____

_____

Contractions

Choose the right bee for the flower. Which contraction correctly combines the two words?

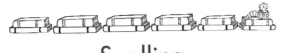

Spelling

Use the words in the box to fill in the blanks. Use each word only once.

Homophones		Other words		Verb spotlight
here	hear	young	morning	fly
bear	bare	pulled	angles	flew
way	weigh	magnify	cone	flying
				flies

Which <u>other words</u> have more than one syllable?

_____   _____   _____

Which of the <u>homophones</u> means *this place*?   Which can mean *listen*?

_____   _____

Which of the <u>homophones</u> is an animal?   Which means *naked*?

_____   _____

Which of the <u>homophones</u> can tell where to go? Which finds out *how heavy*?

_____   _____

Which <u>other word</u> is past tense?

_____

Write the remaining two <u>other words</u>.

_____   _____

Use a <u>verb spotlight</u> verb in a sentence that ends with an exclamation point.

_____

_____

Writing

I woke up, looked out my window, and saw this. What happened next? Use lots of adjectives!

_____

_____

_____

_____

_____

Adjectives and Synonyms

Read each sentence and underline the adjective. Then rewrite the sentence using the **synonym** or similar word for the adjective from the word box. For example, if the original sentence was *The windows are dirty*, *dirty* would be the adjective and *filthy* could be a synonym. Your new sentence would be *The windows are filthy*.

freezing	noisy	fantastic	soaked	quick
delighted	lengthy	scratchy	delicious	glistening

This road is long. _____

My music is loud. _____

The road is wet. _____

That car was fast. _____

The baby is happy. _____

It is cold outside. _____

The sandpaper is rough. _____

That concert was excellent! _____

The snack was yummy. _____

The shiny diamond sparkled. _____

Writing

Imagine you saw a van so full of bananas they were spilling out the door. Write a story about what happened. Where did the van come from? Where was it going? Why were there so many bananas?

_____

_____

_____

_____

_____

_____

_____

_____

_____

Compound Words

Connect the words on the left to the words on the right to make compound words.
At the bottom, make your own compound words by filling in the blanks.

out	ways
cow	ball
back	bow
rain	side
side	fly
butter	father
race	set
base	time
sun	yard
lunch	car
grand	boy

sail_____   sand_____

straw_____   cup_____

Spelling

Use the words in the box to fill in the blanks. Use each word only once.

Homophones		Other words		Verb spotlight
flower	flour	sugar	it's	smell
bored	board	being	orbit	smelled
hair	hare	leave	position	smelling
				smells

Which <u>other words</u> have more than one syllable?

_____   _____   _____

_____

Which of the <u>homophones</u> is a plant?   Which is a bread ingredient?

_____   _____

Which of the <u>homophones</u> means *uninterested*?   Which is a plank of wood?

_____   _____

Which of the <u>homophones</u> grows on your head?   Which is a rabbit?

_____   _____

Which <u>other word</u> is a contraction?   Which is a synonym of *depart*?

_____   _____

Use a <u>verb spotlight</u> verb in a sentence that ends with an exclamation point.

_____

_____

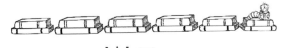

Writing

Write directions for how to play Simon Says. Start with explaining what you are giving directions for. Include how to play, rules of the game, and how to win.

_____

_____

_____

_____

_____

_____

Describe with Adjectives

Study this picture. Then use descriptive words to explain what you see. Be specific! Read your description to a family member and see if they can draw what you have described. What could you change to make your description even more specific?

_____

_____

_____

_____

_____

_____

Writing

What happens next? Choose a book you are reading now, or a favorite book, and write what happens next in the story.

_____

_____

_____

_____

_____

_____

Writing

Choose five items in the room with you. Describe each with five adjectives. If you can describe one of them with ten adjectives, get a high five and/or a hug.

1. _____

_____

2. _____

_____

3. _____

_____

4. _____

_____

5. _____

_____

Spelling

Use the words in the box to fill in the blanks. Use each word only once.

ur sound words		Other words		Verb spotlight
curled	firm	polygon	clear	visit
church	skirt	experiment	noun	visited
perfect	person	cylinder	verb	visiting
				visits

Put the ur sound words in alphabetical order.

_____   _____   _____

_____   _____   _____

Which word has four syllables?

_____

Which other words are shapes?

_____   _____

Which other words are parts of speech?

_____   _____

Write the remaining other word.

_____

Use a verb spotlight verb in a question that contains adjectives.

_____

_____

Short Story - Setup

In the first box, make a list of three types of people or animals. One of these will be your **character**, who your story will be about. In the second box, make a list of three places. One of these will be your **setting**, where your story takes place. In the third box, write three problems. One of these will become your **plot**, what your story is about.

Character

Setting

Plot

(continued on the next page)

Short Story – Writing

Choose one thing from each list and write a short story using those story elements: the **character**, the **setting**, and the **plot**.

_____

_____

_____

_____

_____

_____

_____

_____

_____

_____

Adjectives and Nouns

In each sentence, underline the adjective. Then on the line beside the sentence, write the noun that is being described by the adjective.

I wore an itchy sweater to school. _____

My sister wants a miniature pony. _____

The wild animals made some noise. _____

The noisy kids sounded like animals. _____

The delicious candy is gone. _____

Our church has an expensive piano. _____

The colorful robe is on the hanger. _____

My mom has such beautiful eyes. _____

My aunt has long hair. _____

The movie was boring. _____

My brother is sick. _____

Short Story – Writing

Choose a new thing from each list on your page from lesson 97 and write a new short story using those story elements: the **character**, the **setting**, and the **plot**.

_____

_____

_____

_____

_____

_____

_____

_____

_____

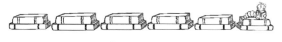
Writing

Make a list of ten nouns. Now write the most interesting adjective that you can think of for each of them. They can be outrageous if you like!

1. _____

2. _____

3. _____

4. _____

5. _____

6. _____

7. _____

8. _____

9. _____

10. _____

Spelling

Use the words in the box to fill in the blanks. Use each word only once.

Double consonant words		Other words		Verb spotlight
hugged	happy	evidence	burned	talk
correct	different	opinion	conduct	talked
funny	error	likely	certain	talking
				talks

Which <u>double consonant words</u> have two syllables?

_____   _____   _____

_____

Which <u>double consonant word</u> has one syllable?   Which has three syllables?

_____   _____

Which <u>other words</u> start with a vowel?

_____   _____

Which <u>other word</u> starts with a *hard c*?   Which starts with a *soft c*?

_____   _____

Which word is a synonym for *probable*?   Which is in the past tense?

_____   _____

Use a <u>verb spotlight</u> verb in a statement.

_____

_____

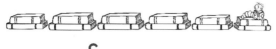

Summary

Read the short story by Jenn Appel below and then summarize it. Write the main idea of the story in the big oval with supporting ideas in the ovals below it.

The only thing Bristol had in mind that morning when she woke was going sledding. She rushed to do her morning chores — washing dishes, picking up her room, cleaning off the table, and starting laundry. She made quick work of all her jobs before begging her mother to go sledding.

Her mother was thrilled to see Bristol had finished all her chores without having to be told. She told her to get ready to sled. Bristol put on her snow pants, boots, coat, gloves, and hat. She grabbed her orange sled, and the two of them walked hand in hand towards the hill, both happy for the beautiful day ahead of them.

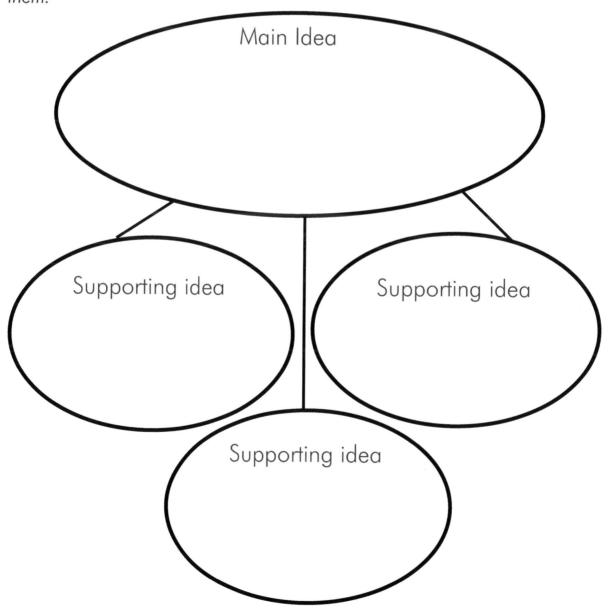

Main Idea

Supporting idea

Supporting idea

Supporting idea

Adjectives and Nouns

In each sentence, underline the adjective. Then on the line beside the sentence, write the noun that is being described by the adjective.

The giant spider scared me.   _____

My dad takes me on big adventures.   _____

The exotic bird was squawking.   _____

The blonde woman left her purse.   _____

The gray clouds gave way to rain.   _____

The hungry cat waited for his food.   _____

The bouncy ball hit the ceiling.   _____

My favorite shoes are missing.   _____

My dog is so fluffy after his bath.   _____

Our mailman is very friendly.   _____

The fussy baby woke me up.   _____

Writing

Write a postcard. Where are you writing from? Home? The moon? Somewhere else?

Prefixes and Suffixes

Break each of the words up into prefix, base word, and suffix.

unsuccessful

Prefix: _____   Base word: _____   Suffix: _____

biweekly

Prefix: _____   Base word: _____   Suffix: _____

unthinkable

Prefix: _____   Base word: _____   Suffix: _____

insightful

Prefix: _____   Base word: _____   Suffix: _____

misunderstanding

Prefix: _____   Base word: _____   Suffix: _____

inconceivable

Prefix: _____   Base word: _____   Suffix: _____

Spelling

Use the words in the box to fill in the blanks. Use each word only once.

Compound words		Other words		Verb spotlight
notebook	football	future	sphere	sing
bookcase	hallway	forecast	highest	sang
classroom	outdoors	conclusion	pyramid	singing
				sings

Put the <u>compound words</u> in alphabetical order.

_____   _____   _____

_____   _____   _____

Which <u>other words</u> have three syllables?

_____   _____

Which unused <u>other word</u> is a shape?   Which can be a weather word?

_____   _____

Which word is a synonym for *upcoming*?   Which is a synonym for *utmost*?

_____   _____

Use a <u>verb spotlight</u> verb in a statement and another in a question.

_____

_____

_____

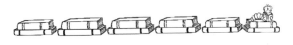

Story Summary

Read the following short story by Jenn Appel. Then write a summary of the story.

Do you know what the fastest animal in the world is? If you answered cheetah, you're right. However, a cheetah can only run quickly for less than half of a mile before being too exhausted to continue. If a cheetah were in a mile-long race, it would lose to a pronghorn.

A pronghorn is sometimes mistaken for an antelope but is more related to the goat family. These unique animals can sustain speeds of around thirty miles an hour for twenty miles! Try to get a cheetah to do that, and you'll be quickly disappointed.

Next time someone asks you to run like a cheetah, remember the pronghorn and try to run like it instead.

What is the **main idea** of the story? Write one complete sentence that tells the story's main idea.

_____

_____

What are the **most important things** that happened in the story? Write one or two complete sentences that tell the story's most important things.

_____

_____

Story Summary

Read this short story. Then write a summary of the story.

A unique type of cloud, the lenticular cloud, is frequently mistaken for a UFO. These special clouds form above a mountain, a tall building, or other large object that can obstruct air flow. A slight wind creates waves on the side of the object opposite the direction of the wind. Given the right temperatures, the moisture in the air condenses to produce a strange, saucer-shaped cloud. Lenticular clouds can actually be quite dangerous for pilots of powered aircraft due to the turbulence created above them. Interestingly though, glider pilots use the turbulence to their advantage. In fact, the world records for both distance and altitude of a glider were set utilizing the turbulence of lenticular clouds.

What is the **main idea** of the story? Write one complete sentence that tells the story's main idea.

_____

_____

What are the **most important things** that happened in the story? Write one or two complete sentences that tell the story's most important things.

_____

_____

_____

Story Summary

Read this abridged Aesop's Fable, "The Fox and the Crow." Write a summary.

One bright morning as the Fox was following his sharp nose through the wood in search of a bite to eat, he saw a Crow on the limb of a tree overhead. This lucky Crow held a bit of cheese in her beak.

"No need to search any farther," thought sly Master Fox. "Here is a dainty bite for my breakfast."

Up he trotted to the foot of the tree in which the Crow was sitting, and looking up admiringly, he cried, "Good-morning, beautiful creature!"

The Crow, her head cocked on one side, watched the Fox suspiciously. But she kept her beak tightly closed on the cheese and did not return his greeting.

"What a charming creature she is!" said the Fox. "How her feathers shine! What a beautiful form and what splendid wings! Could she sing just one song, I know I should hail her Queen of Birds."

Listening to these flattering words, the Crow forgot all her suspicion, and also her breakfast. She wanted very much to be called Queen of Birds.

So she opened her beak wide to utter her loudest caw, and down fell the cheese straight into the Fox's open mouth.

_____

_____

_____

_____

_____

Story Summary

Read this Greek myth. Then write a summary of what you read.

Daedalus was an architect and inventor. His son was Icarus. They lived on the Isle of Crete but wished to return to their home in Athens. Being a fabulous inventor, Daedalus created a pair of artificial wings that allowed Icarus and himself to fly. He made the wings out of feathers held tightly together by wax.

As they began their journey home, Daedalus warned Icarus not to fly too high. This would cause him to get too close to the sun, melting the wax that held his wings together. Unfortunately, Icarus ignored his father's instructions. His wings melted and he plummeted into the Mediterranean Sea.

_____

_____

_____

_____

_____

Spelling

Use the words in the box to fill in the blanks. Use each word only once.

-ful/-fully words		Other words		Verb spotlight
beautiful	thankfully	feature	basket	empty
cheerful	joyfully	history	welcome	emptied
useful	helpfully	advantage	until	emptying
				empties

Which words outside of the <u>verb spotlight</u> have three syllables?

_____   _____   _____

_____   _____   _____

Which remaining words outside of the <u>verb spotlight</u> start with a vowel?

_____   _____

Which word is a synonym for *happy*?   Which word can mean *aspect*?

_____   _____

Which word can be a greeting?   Which word is a container?

_____   _____

Use a <u>verb spotlight</u> verb in a dialogue with two quotation sentences.

_____

_____

_____

_____

Spelling

See if you can spell each of the words represented by the pictures below on the lines beside them.

_____   _____

_____   _____

_____   _____

_____   _____

_____   _____

_____   _____

_____   _____

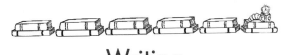

Writing

Write a summary of a story or chapter you read for school. Write the main idea and a couple of supporting details. Make sure you tell the problem and how it was solved.

_____

_____

_____

_____

_____

_____

_____

_____

Main Idea and Details

Read the paragraphs and answer the questions about them.

Main ideas are what the paragraph or story is about. Sometimes they are stated (usually in the first sentence of a paragraph). Sometimes they are unstated and are more of a summary of the whole paragraph.

What is the main idea of this paragraph?
   a. Sometimes main ideas are stated.
   b. Main ideas are what the paragraph or story is about.
   c. Sometimes main ideas are unstated.

Emma, Miley, and Kara had a fun day at the pool. They played water polo while giggling and splashing. They did flips off of the diving board. They laid out in the warm sun to soak up the vitamin D. They were glad for a day of fun in the sun.

What is the main idea of this paragraph?
   a. Emma, Miley, and Kara had a fun day at the pool.
   b. They played water polo while giggling and splashing.
   c. They laid out in the warm sun.

Why did they lay out in the warm sun?
   a. They were glad for a day of fun in the sun.
   b. They wanted to soak up the vitamin D.
   c. They wanted to have a fun day at the pool.

Fruits and vegetables have lots of vitamins and minerals. They can boost your immune system and help you avoid sickness. They increase energy and leave you feeling alert.

What is the main idea of this paragraph?
   a. Fruits and vegetables have lots of vitamins and minerals.
   b. They increase energy and leave you feeling alert.
   c. There are many benefits to fruits and vegetables.

Why do fruits and vegetables leave you feeling alert?
   a. They have lots of vitamins and minerals.
   b. They increase energy.
   c. They can boost your immune system.

Verb Vacancy

There's a verb vacancy! Help match the subjects to the correct *to be* verbs.

babies

are   am

boy

was   were

trains

are   is

blanket

am   is

door

was   were

stove

am   is

she

is   are

dog

was   am

snake

is   are

teacher

are   is

TV

was   were

chair

is   were

girls

are   is

you

was   were

Jane

was   were

mailman

is   are

Spelling

Use the words in the box to fill in the blanks. Use each word only once.

Contractions		Other Words		Verb Spotlight
didn't	haven't	natural	pretty	pass
you're	she's	climate	cycle	passed
we're	they're	federal	lunar	passing
				passes

Put the <u>other words</u> in alphabetical order.

_____   _____   _____

_____   _____   _____

Which contractions stand for a pair of words with *not* in them?

_____   _____

Which contractions stand for a pair of words with *are* in them?

_____   _____   _____

Which contraction stands for a pair of words with *is* in them?

_____

Use a <u>verb spotlight</u> verb in an exclamation and a statement.

_____

_____

_____

Main Idea and Details

Read the paragraphs and answer the questions about them.

The jungle can be an exciting place. There are so many different kinds of plants and animals. It can rain with little to no warning. The bright, vivid colors are breathtaking.

What is the main idea of this paragraph?
    a. The colors are bright and vivid.
    b. There are many plants and animals.
    c. The jungle can be an exciting place.

I love going to the beach. The salty sea air is so refreshing. The thundering sound of the waves crashing against the shore is music to my ears. Also, who doesn't love the feel of sand between their toes?

What is the main idea of this paragraph?
    a. Everyone loves the feel of sand.
    b. I love going to the beach.
    c. Salty air is refreshing.

Which of the following details supports the main idea?
    a. The salty sea air is so refreshing.
    b. Waves make a thundering sound.
    c. I have sand between my toes.

We can survive much longer without food than we can without water. Our bodies are made up primarily of water. We lose much fluid through evaporation, perspiration, and urination, and it needs to be replenished.

What is the main idea of this paragraph?
    a. We lose fluid that needs to be replenished.
    b. Our bodies are made up of water.
    c. Water is important for our bodies.

Why does fluid need to be replenished?
    a. Our bodies are made up primarily of water.
    b. We can survive much longer without food than without water.
    c. We lose much fluid through evaporation, perspiration, and urination.

Adjectives and Nouns

In each sentence, fill in the blank with an adjective that fits the sentence. Then underline the noun being described.

The shirt that I wore was _____.

The dishes on the counter are _____.

The ring on her finger was _____.

The girl's hair was _____.

The cake was _____.

She had _____ gum stuck in her hair.

The _____ water refreshed the athletes.

The _____ crash startled them all.

His _____ nose needs a tissue.

The cantata was _____.

My dog looks _____.

Writing

Write a summary of the chapter or story you read for school today (or recently). Include a main idea sentence and a couple of supporting details. A summary should probably include the character, the setting, what problem is faced, and how they are trying to fix the problem.

_____

_____

_____

_____

_____

_____

_____

Verb Vacancy

Fill in the blank with the correct *present tense* verb form of the word in parentheses. Remember that present tense words happen today.

The babies _____ when they are hungry.
(to cry)

The snake _____ at the predator.
(to hiss)

The boy _____ with his ball at the park.
(to play)

The teacher _____ the class with patience.
(to teach)

The trains _____ along the tracks.
(to chug)

The TV _____ in the next room.
(to blare)

The blanket _____ my cold feet.
(to cover)

The chair _____ the sitting child.
(to hold)

The girls _____ on the roller coaster.
(to scream)

Comparative Adjectives

Adjectives that are used to compare two things are called **comparative adjectives**. *Smarter*, *more colorful*, *happier*, and *less* are all examples of comparative adjectives. Write the comparative form of the following adjectives:

peaceful _____   clean _____

crazy _____   excited _____

young _____   strong _____

angry _____   happy _____

quiet _____   wet _____

green _____   scared _____

big _____   brave _____

bad _____   far _____

silly _____   good _____

dirty _____   pretty _____

easy _____   healthy _____

boring _____   friendly _____

sweet _____   safe _____

high _____   thin _____

busy _____   short _____

large _____   dry _____

early _____   hot _____

Homophones

Homophones are words that sound alike but have different spellings and/or meanings. For each sentence below, underline the homophone that best fits the sentence. Learn from any mistakes you make.

The ___ outside is frightful.	weather	whether
___ mom is running late.	They're	Their
The criminal tried to ___ the scene.	flea	flee
We sang an old ___ at church.	hymn	him
Cover your eyes and don't ___.	peak	peek
We ___ our bikes home.	rode	road
The story is a ___ about ponies.	tail	tale

Homonyms

Homonyms are words that sound the same and have the same spelling but have different meanings. Read each sentence and fill in the homonym in the blank.

can hit a ball or fly around at night   _____

a group putting on a show or a hard
bandage to protect broken bones   _____

a type of bug or the zipper on pants   _____

a kind of drink or to hit with your fist   _____

Superlative Adjectives

Adjectives that are used to show the highest or lowest ranking among things are called **superlative adjectives**. *Smartest*, *most colorful*, *happiest*, and *least* are all examples of superlative adjectives. Write the superlative form of the following adjectives:

careful _____   dirty _____

scary _____   curious _____

old _____   cold _____

sad _____   dry _____

long _____   red _____

curly _____   close _____

thin _____   quiet _____

excited _____   large _____

good _____   happy _____

easy _____   bad _____

pretty _____   busy _____

big _____   early _____

sweet _____   far _____

silly _____   scared _____

brave _____   friendly _____

high _____   young _____

Main Idea

Read the paragraphs and choose the main idea of each one.

Soccer is known as the easiest sport in the world. At its core, all you need to know is you are attempting to get the ball into the other team's goal without using your hands. What could be easier?

What is the main idea of this paragraph?
  a. Soccer is easy.
  b. Soccer is fun.
  c. Soccer doesn't allow hands.

Cockroaches can go without food for up to six weeks at a time. In addition, they can eat almost anything, including glue and hair. They can live for weeks without their heads and are very quick. All of these things make cockroaches difficult to control in our homes.

What is the main idea of this paragraph?
  a. Cockroaches don't need a lot of food.
  b. Cockroaches are quick.
  c. Cockroaches are hard to control.

Ladybugs are a colorful kind of beetle. Most of them are red with black spots. However, some are black with red spots. There are even some with orange or yellow wings!

What is the main idea of this paragraph?
  a. Ladybugs are usually red.
  b. Ladybugs come in many colors.
  c. Ladybugs can be orange or yellow.

An average of 3,000 vehicles are crushed each year at Monster Truck rallies. Organizers get the vehicles from local junkyards and return them when the rallies are over. Cars, vans, and even planes are crushed by the giant trucks.

What is the main idea of this paragraph? Write it on the line.

_____

Writing

Write a summary of the chapter or story you read for school today (or recently). What's the main topic? If you can, write your summary in one sentence. You'll have to use words like *and* or *but*. If you can write your summary in one sentence, get a high five and/or hug.

_____

_____

_____

_____

_____

Comparative or Superlative

For each sentence, fill in the **comparative** (comparing two things) or **superlative** (highest or lowest rank among a series of things) form of the adjective in the blank. The last one is tricky. Can you figure it out?

My dad is _(strong)_ than yours. _____

Your sister is the _(happy)_ little girl. _____

Jeff is _(hungry)_ than James. _____

Canada is _(peaceful)_ than Syria. _____

Her feet are the _(small)_ I've seen. _____

My room is _(clean)_ than yours. _____

That's the _(big)_ snowball ever. _____

The last clown was the _(silly)_. _____

Her hair is the _(beautiful)_ of all. _____

The earth is _(small)_ than Jupiter. _____

The swings are _(fun)_ than the slide. _____

Rhode Island is the _(small)_ state. _____

Her score was the _(good)_ all year. _____

Paragraph Writing

Use the hamburger below to help you write a paragraph. Today, come up with your main idea and two supporting details for that main idea. You will complete this in lesson 129.

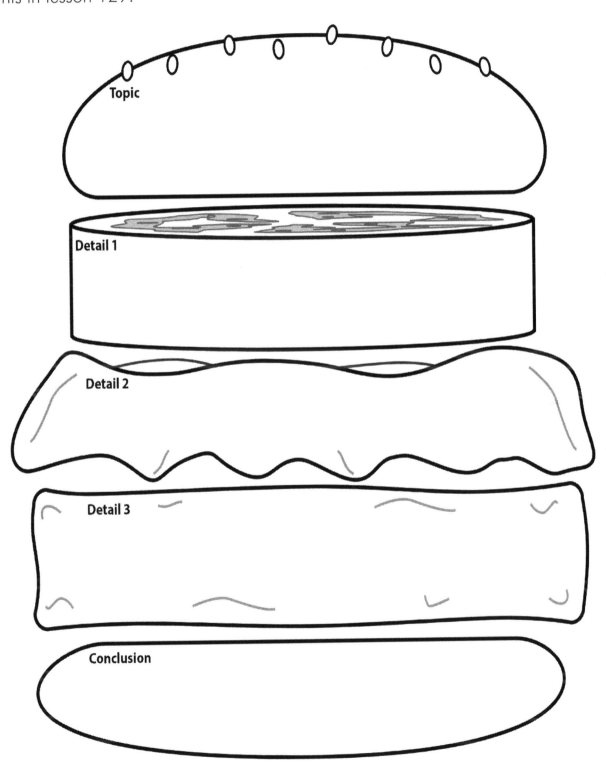

Topic

Detail 1

Detail 2

Detail 3

Conclusion

Comparative and Superlative Adjectives

In each sentence, underline the comparative or superlative adjective. Then on the line beside the sentence, write the things that are being compared.

She was the prettiest girl in school. _____

The doll was bigger than the teacup. _____

July was the hottest month of the year. _____

Friday was colder than Saturday. _____

The rose is the most beautiful flower. _____

Water is more beneficial than soda. _____

It was the longest book I've ever read. _____

Black is darker than pink. _____

Your car is faster than mine. _____

My grandpa's car is the slowest. _____

My dog's hair is fluffiest after a bath. _____

Paragraph Writing

Finish your hamburger from lesson 127. Flip back to that page or use this one if you prefer. You need one more supporting detail and a conclusion.

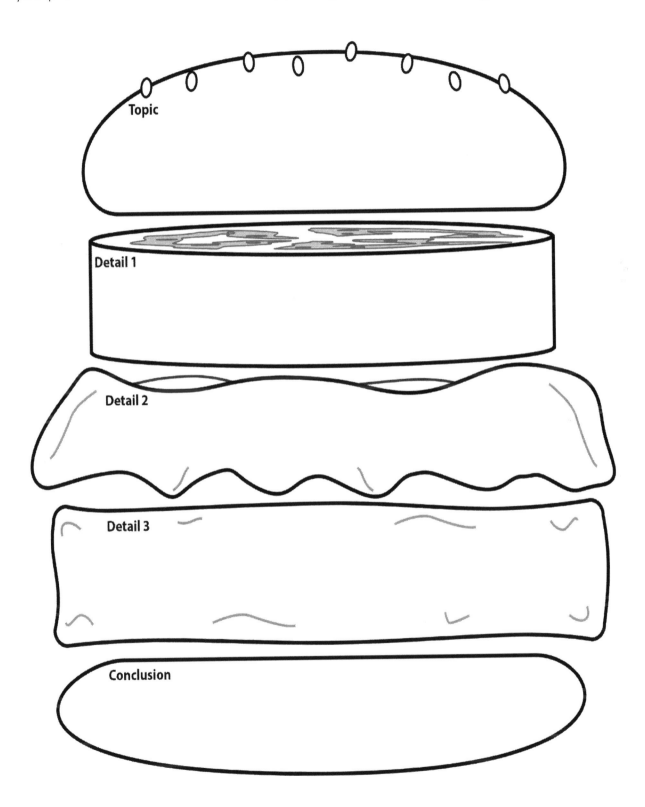

Topic

Detail 1

Detail 2

Detail 3

Conclusion

Verb Vacancy

There's a verb vacancy! Help match the subjects to the correct *past tense* verbs.

Last week, the wind
blew.   blown.

Yesterday, you
runned.   ran.

Last month, the door
shut.   shutted.

Last year, we
helps.   helped.

A few hours ago, I
drunk.   drank.

Last week, the chair
held.   holded.

Yesterday, the tree
fell.   fallen.

Last month, the boy
thrown.   threw.

Last year, Jane
sung.   sang.

A few hours ago, she
read.   readed.

Last week, the man
yell.   yelled.

Yesterday, the dog
chased.   chases.

Last month, we all
goed.   went.

Last year, Joseph
weeped.   wept.

A few hours ago, he
came.   comed.

Last week, the swing
swang.   swung.

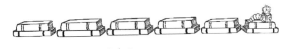

Writing

Write your **paragraph** (from lessons 127 and 129) by hand. Indent your first word and copy your sentences from your hamburger(s). Write each sentence right after the one before it. DON'T start each sentence on a new line.

Interesting Sentences

Can you make a sentence more interesting? By adding adjectives and adverbs, being more specific, and answering the question where or why, you can turn a sentence like *The dog played* into *The large golden retriever frolicked enthusiastically in the backyard.* Make the following sentences more interesting.

The girls read.

_____

_____

The boys sat.

_____

_____

Now write your own interesting sentence. Ask yourself the following questions to make your sentence better: How can I be more specific with my nouns and verbs? What kind? How? Where? Why? What details and interesting words can I add?

_____

_____

Writing

Write two complete sentences. They can be about anything you'd like.

_____

_____

_____

_____

Now, turn them into a **compound sentence**, one that takes two sentences and combines them with a comma and a **conjunction** (and, but, or).

_____

_____

_____

Paragraph Writing

Fill in this hamburger for a paragraph summary of a chapter you've read. What's the topic, or main idea, of the chapter? You will have a topic or main idea sentence, three supporting detail sentences, and a closing sentence about the topic. Can you use at least one compound sentence?

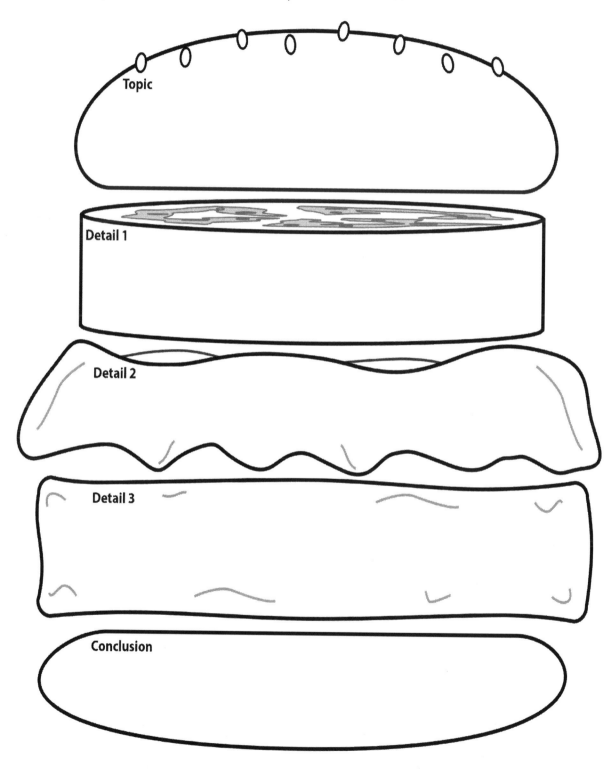

Topic

Detail 1

Detail 2

Detail 3

Conclusion

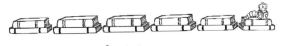

Verb Vacancy

There's a verb vacancy! Fill in the blank with the correct *past participle* verbs.

The trains have _____ into the station.
(went/gone)

The girl had _____ away from the dog.
(ran/run)

The tree had _____ in the forest.
(fallen/fell)

The wind must have _____ it over.
(blown/blew)

We had _____ all the punch.
(drank/drunk)

The pitcher had _____ the ball.
(threw/thrown)

The catcher had _____ it.
(caught/catched)

The boys have _____ their game.
(finish/finished)

Spelling

Use the words in the box to fill in the blanks. Use each word only once.

-er words		Other words		Verb spotlight
under	fever	state	main	dance
whether	never	interaction	explorer	danced
answer	border	swim	prior	dancing
				dances

Put the <u>other words</u> in alphabetical order.

_____   _____   _____

_____   _____   _____

Which <u>–er word</u> is an antonym for *always*?   Which is a synonym for *beneath*?

_____

Which <u>–er word</u> is a homophone of *weather*?   Which can mean *reply*?

_____

Which <u>–er word</u> can indicate sickness?   Write the last <u>–er word</u>.

_____

Use a <u>verb spotlight</u> verb in two statements that include adjectives.

_____

_____

_____

Writing

Use your hamburger from lesson 134 and put your sentences together. Write your paragraph.

_____

_____

_____

_____

_____

_____

_____

Main Idea

Read the paragraphs and find the main idea of each.

Oranges are a fantastic source of vitamin C. They have lots of dietary fiber and other vitamins as well. The calcium in oranges make them an all-around great snack choice.

What is the main idea of this paragraph?
   a. Oranges are a fantastic source of vitamin C.
   b. Oranges are a good snack choice.
   c. There are many health benefits to oranges.

Did you know that there are more than 5,000 species of frogs? Some frogs can jump over twenty times their own body length. Have you ever seen a frog drink water? They actually don't need to because they absorb water through their skin!

What is the main idea of this paragraph?
   a. There are lots of interesting frog facts.
   b. Frogs don't need to drink water.
   c. Frogs can jump far.

Are you feeling a little sluggish? It seems ridiculous, but getting some exercise can actually give you energy. Get up and take a walk, jog in place, or do some jumping jacks. Don't skip breakfast either. Fueling your body can increase your energy. Drinking more water can also help your body reenergize.

What is the main idea of this paragraph?
   a. Water gives you energy.
   b. There are different ways to increase energy.
   c. Exercise gives you energy.

Summer is a great time of year. The weather is warm, pools are open, and vacations abound. Of course, fall is great, too. The crisp air, apples, pumpkins, and hayrides are all fun. Winter is so beautiful with its snowy landscapes and cozy sweaters. Spring is full of new life, flowers, butterflies, and color. Who could pick a favorite?

What is the main idea of this paragraph? Write it on the line.

Writing

Write a paragraph summary of a chapter you've read. What's the main idea of the chapter? Remember, you need five sentences. You need a main idea sentence, three supporting detail sentences, and a closing sentence about the topic.

_____

_____

_____

_____

_____

_____

_____

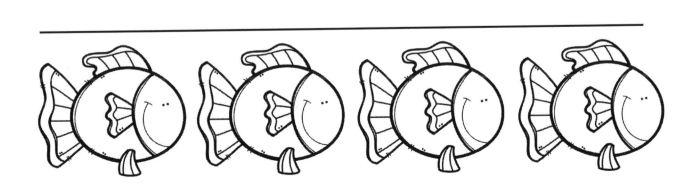

Vowel Pairing

Use the apples to pick the vowels that are missing from each word.

coff____
ui oa ea ee

b____t
oi ea ui ie

b____k
ea ui ee ie

fl____s
oi ie ui oa

p____ple
ui oi eo oa

expl____n
ie ee oa ai

bel____ve
oo ee ie ai

g____st
ue ui oo ie

fr____nd
oo ui oe ie

g____ng
ea oi ai ui

bl____ch
ie ea ai ie

c____ld
ea ee ou oi

ar____nd
ui ie ou ea

id____
oo ie oa ea

gr____n
oo oa oe ie

sq____rm
ea oi ai ui

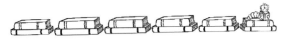

Spelling

Use the words in the box to fill in the blanks. Use each word only once.

-le/-al words		Other words		Verb spotlight
total	chuckle	infer	knowledge	wrap
signal	giggle	modify	sequence	wrapped
central	candle	doesn't	comprehend	wrapping
				wraps

Put the -le/-al words in alphabetical order.

_____   _____   _____

_____   _____   _____

Which other words have three syllables?

_____   _____

Which other word is a contraction?   Which means *assume*?

_____   _____

Which other word is a synonym for *order*?   Which can mean *intelligence*?

_____   _____

Use a verb spotlight verb in a statement and question that each use a quotation.

_____

_____

_____

Simple, Compound, and Complex Sentences

Make **compound sentences** using *and, but, or.* Use each conjunction once to combine the given sentences with another sentence that you create.

The dress is pretty. _____

_____

The dog is muddy. _____

_____

Should I eat this cold soup? _____

_____

Make **complex sentences** by adding each of *when, if, because* to make these sentences longer by adding a **clause**, a group of words with a subject and verb.

The phone rang, but we didn't hear it. _____

_____

I like lettuce, and I like tomatoes, too. _____

_____

We can watch a movie. _____

_____

Simple, Compound, and Complex Sentences

Decide whether the following sentences are simple, compound, or complex by underlining your answer.

The bridge was crowded with cars.

      simple   compound   complex

I went to the eye doctor, and he said I need glasses.

      simple   compound   complex

You can do anything if you put your mind to it.

      simple   compound   complex

Please park your bike in the garage.

      simple   compound   complex

Her laugh was infectious.

      simple   compound   complex

Put the letter in the box after you put a stamp on it.

      simple   compound   complex

The boy, a sixth grader, was embarrassed.

      simple   compound   complex

I wanted to take a nap, but I ran out of time.

      simple   compound   complex

Writing

Write a simple sentence, a compound sentence, and a complex sentence. For a complex sentence you could add *because*, *if*, or *when*. Include an adjective in each sentence. Each sentence type is described below if you need a reminder.

Simple sentence: Expresses a complete thought with one independent clause.

_____

_____

Compound sentence: two or more independent clauses connected by a conjunction.

_____

_____

Complex sentence: an independent clause and at least one dependent clause.

_____

_____

Writing

Write a simple sentence, a compound sentence, and a complex sentence. For a complex sentence you could add *because*, *if*, or *when*. Include an adjective in each sentence. Each sentence type is described below if you need a reminder.

Simple sentence: Expresses a complete thought with one independent clause.

_____

_____

Compound sentence: two or more independent clauses connected by a conjunction.

_____

_____

Complex sentence: an independent clause and at least one dependent clause.

_____

_____

Plurals

Select the correct plural form of each word. On the next section, write each word as a plural on the blank beside it.

miss

misss   miss'   misses   missies

boy

boys   boyes   boies   boy's

fox

foxs   foxes   foxies   foxs'

loss

losss   losses   loss's   lossies

key

keyss   keyes   keys   key's

bone

bons   bonies   bon's   bones

pin

pins   pines   pinies   pinns

hero

heros   heroe   heroes   hero's

bowl _____

swing _____

shoe _____

match _____

candy _____

lamp _____

box _____

toy _____

Conjunctions

Combine the sentences using one of the **conjunctions** or joining words below. There can be more than one answer, so try to use a different word each time.

| and | if | or | because | since | but |

We went to the bank. Then we went to the store.

_____

_____

I like pizza. It tastes good.

_____

Wear your gloves and hat. It is cold outside.

_____

_____

You can have an apple. You can have an orange.

_____

_____

She won first place. She was the best runner.

_____

_____

He wished he could have gone. He was sick.

_____

_____

Conjunctions and Compound Sentences

Choose the option that best completes the sentence, using the conjunction as your clue. Fill in the last sentence yourself.

Pharaoh didn't let the people go although...

    a.   God sent plagues.

    b.   Aaron's staff.

    c.   the Nile River.

    d.   they worked hard.

I don't want to eat that candy because...

    a.   I love candy.

    b.   too sweet.

    c.   I have a dentist appointment later today.

    d.   candy is delicious.

I should go to bed, but...

    a.   I'm tired.

    b.   I can't put my book down!

    c.   it's late.

    d.   it's cold.

I like to sing, and...

    a.   messy room.

    b.   there's a lot of trash.

    c.   turn the light on.

    d.   I like to dance.

Would you like to have a salad, or...

_____

Conjunctions and Compound Sentences

Write five simple sentences below. Once you have written all five, continue with the assignment on the next page.

1. _____

_____

2. _____

_____

3. _____

_____

4. _____

_____

5. _____

_____

(continued on next page)

Conjunctions and Compound Sentences

Combine four of your simple sentences with the first four sentences below using **and, but, or,** and **so.** You will need a comma and then the conjunction you choose. Then combine the last sentence below with your fifth sentence using **because.** Do not use a comma before because. Here are the sentences:

School is fun.

I am tired.

Pizza is my favorite food.

I'm dizzy from spinning.

Playdough is squishy.

_____

_____

_____

_____

_____

_____

_____

Conjunctions and Compound Sentences

Write a sentence with **, and** in the middle of it. Write another sentence with **, but** in the middle of it. Write a third sentence with **, or** in the middle of it. Each side of the conjunction should be an **independent clause** or something that could stand as a sentence on its own.

_____

_____

_____

_____

_____

_____

sentence   conjunction   sentence

Plurals

Use the grid at the top of the page as a Bingo board. The words are in the Parent's Guide. As the words are read to you, place a marker of some kind over the correct plural ending for that word. Get four in a row to win. On the bottom of the page, write the plurals of the words in the blanks beside them.

s	es	s	ies
es	ves	ies	es
ies	s	es	s
ves	es	s	ies

story_____   straw_____

paper_____   bowl_____

turkey_____   arch_____

potato_____   goose_____

mix _____   game_____

Writing

Write a fun story about having a giraffe as a pet. Make sure you use some compound sentences. Get a high five for each compound sentence you use and for each sentence with *because*. Don't use a comma with *because*!

Parts of Speech

Let's review the parts of speech! Color all of the nouns blue. Color all of the verbs green. Color all of the adjectives red.

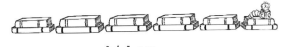

Writing

Write a short story called, "Where Is My _____?" Decide what is lost and write about the things you did to find it.

_____

_____

_____

_____

_____

_____

_____

_____

_____

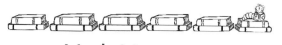

Verb Vacancy

Choose the correct verb for each subject.

The cat
was   were

The players
have   has

The girls
is   are

The game
was   were

The laundry
have   has

The pillow
is   are

The skates
was   were

You
has   have

I
am   are

They
am   are

The board
has   have

The toys
was   were

The snacks
has   have

The shirt
is   are

The boy
was   were

The mom
has   have

Plurals

Write the correct plurals for each of these words. Remember that some just don't follow any rules!

flake _____   drop _____

man _____   train _____

fly _____   mouse_____

mess _____   tomato _____

belly _____   tree _____

fox _____   beach_____

deer _____   glass _____

radio _____   donkey _____

Writing

Choose a line from each box and put them together to form the instructions for your writing assignment.

Write a story about	a silly	chimpanzee in the circus.
Describe an adventure with	a grumpy	train conductor on a break.
Write a letter to	a careless	toy soldier in a parade.

_____

_____

_____

_____

_____

_____

_____

Parts of Speech

Let's review the parts of speech! Color all of the nouns blue. Color all of the verbs green. Color all of the adjectives red.

spoke wore poster cabinet

yummy burly picking

food long arm he

was striped gave

caught glove good special

write tree savory

sudden pie pink easy

Spelling

Write your spelling words on the lines below as they are read to you from the Parent's Guide. Learn from any spelling mistakes you make.

Homophones

Find the homophone of each word by choosing a word from the box and writing it on the line.

bee	by	right	red	flour	no	there	bear
maid	pear	not	close	piece	steel	groan	
waste	some	tail	merry	so	berry	meet	

marry_____   read_____

sew_____   meat_____

bare_____   know_____

buy_____   write_____

knot_____   bury_____

grown_____   flower_____

pair_____   made_____

waist_____   tale_____

Plurals

Write the correct plurals for each of these words. Remember that some just don't follow any rules!

rake _____   clock _____

woman _____   giant _____

cry _____   cactus _____

loss _____   piano _____

cherry _____   bee _____

tax _____   punch _____

spy _____   class _____

hero _____   monkey _____

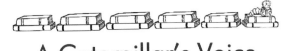

A Caterpillar's Voice

Circle the letter that best completes the word in the sentence.

A frightening animal was in the ___are's den.   **h sc bl**

The animal's voice ___ared out.   **h sc bl**

All of the other animals were ___ared.   **h sc bl**

Fill in the blanks with words from the word box to complete the story.

day	cave	brave	scary
	saving	afraid	

A caterpillar crawled into the hare's _____.

He used the echo in the cave to make himself sound

like a big, _____ animal. All of the other

animals were _____ to go into the cave. The

frog, though, was very _____. He ended

up _____ the _____.

Parts of Speech

Read the sentences below and figure out what part of speech would fill in the blank. Figure out a word that would make sense and then decide if that word is a noun, verb, or adjective.

The kids wanted to _____ before bed.

adjective   noun   verb

It takes a _____ person to accept criticism.

adjective   noun   verb

The _____ sang a lullaby.

adjective   noun   verb

The _____ ran down the street.

adjective   noun   verb

The dog was _____, so he ate all his dinner.

adjective   noun   verb

I _____ it hard to contain my excitement.

adjective   noun   verb

Writing

Write about a time when you were either scared or brave.

_____

_____

_____

_____

_____

_____

_____

_____

_____

Writing

Write a paragraph about how living in a cave is different from living in a house.

Spelling

Choose the letters from the box that complete the words. Some of the choices are used more than once.

| are | air | err | oa | ow | ou | ur | ir |

c_____cus

ch_____

ch_____ch

squ_____

c_____

h_____

cl_____d

b_____

ch_____y

b_____t

Final Project

You are going to be writing a play, a story that is acted out. Today, make a list of characters that your play will be about. Draw a picture of each character and write their name and some words to describe them.

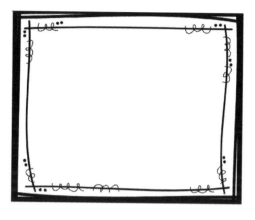

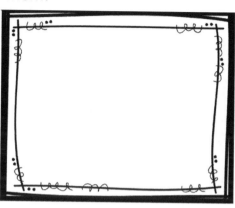

_____

_____

_____

_____

_____

_____

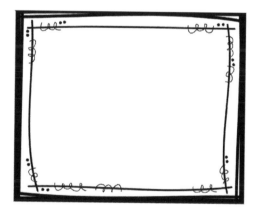

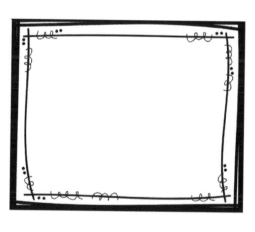

_____

_____

_____

_____

_____

_____

Final Project

Where is your play going to take place? Inside? Outside? On the moon? In a house, a church, or a store? At a park, a race track, the beach, a mountain? Decide on a setting and describe it here. Draw a picture in the box.

_____

_____

_____

_____

_____

Final Project

What is your play going to be about? What is the story going to be? What problem is your main character going to have? Did your character lose something and need to find it? Does your main character need to get somewhere but doesn't know how? What ideas do you have? Write them here.

_____

_____

_____

_____

_____

_____

_____

_____

Final Project

Fill in the sections below on character, setting, and plot.

Who are your **characters**? Write them here:

_____

_____

_____

What is your **setting**? Where and when does your play take place? Will there be other settings? Write them here:

_____

_____

_____

What is your **plot**? What are some problems your characters will face? Write them here:

_____

_____

_____

Final Project

Fill in this story map with information about your **plot**.

Problem

Beginning: What is going to create the problem?

_____

_____

_____

_____

Middle: How are they going to try to solve the problem and fail? What other problems are going to make it worse?

_____

_____

_____

_____

_____

_____

End: How will the problem be solved?

_____

_____

_____

Final Project

Begin writing your play. Write the character name. On the next line write what the character says. Write separately what the character does. Use your previous pages to help you get started.

_____

_____

_____

_____

_____

_____

_____

_____

_____

Final Project

Work on writing your play. Today make sure you finish the beginning of your story. Your character should tell what her problem or his goal is.

_____

_____

_____

_____

_____

_____

_____

_____

_____

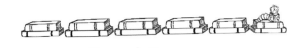
Final Project

Work on writing your play. You should be writing the middle of the play. Use your story map. What different things will your character try to solve his problem or reach her goal? You will work on the middle of your play through lesson 177.

_____

_____

_____

_____

_____

_____

_____

_____

_____

Final Project

Work on writing your play.

_____

_____

_____

_____

_____

_____

_____

_____

_____

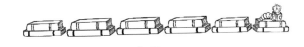

Final Project

Work on writing your play.

_____

_____

_____

_____

_____

_____

_____

_____

Final Project

Work on writing your play. You need to write the end of your play today.

_____

_____

_____

_____

_____

_____

_____

_____

_____

_____

Final Project

Work on writing your play. Wrap up any loose ends.

_____

_____

_____

_____

_____

_____

_____

_____

_____

_____

Final Project

Today you will learn about revising your play.

Ask yourself the following questions:

In the **beginning of the play**:

- Did I talk about the **setting**? Did I tell the reader where and when the story takes place?

- Did I show the **main problem** of the play? Will a reader understand what the problem was?

In the **middle of the play**:

- Did some of my **characters** try to solve the **main problem**? What happened when they tried? Was it clear?

How would I describe the **end of my play**? Circle a choice:

happy   funny   sad   surprising   something else: _____

After you ask yourself these questions, perform these proofreading steps:

- Check that each word is spelled correctly. Look it up if you're not sure.
- Check that each sentence starts with a capital letter and ends with proper punctuation.
- Don't be afraid to ask for help!

If you want to make any changes to your story, do it during the revision process. Think of a change that might make your story more exciting, fun, or interesting. Describe it on the lines below.

_____

_____

Final Project

Read your play to or with your family. Let them leave comments here about their favorite scenes. Great job writing your play!

I liked the story because: _____

_____

My favorite part was: _____

_____

I liked the story because: _____

_____

My favorite part was: _____

_____

I liked the story because: _____

_____

My favorite part was: _____

_____

Congratulations!

You have finished Language Arts 3!

The Easy Peasy All-in-One Homeschool is a free, complete online homeschool curriculum. There are 180 days of ready-to-go assignments for every level and every subject. It's created for your children to work as independently as you want them to. Preschool through high school is available as well as courses ranging from English, math, science and history to art, music, computer, thinking, physical education and health. A daily Bible lesson is offered as well. The mission of Easy Peasy is to enable those to homeschool who otherwise thought they couldn't.

The Genesis Curriculum takes the Bible and turns it into lessons for your homeschool. Daily lessons include Bible reading, memory verse, spelling, handwriting, vocabulary, grammar, Biblical language, science, social studies, writing, and thinking through discussion questions.

The Genesis Curriculum uses a complete book of the Bible for one full year. The curriculum is being made using both Old and New Testament books. Find us online at genesiscurriculum.com to read about the latest developments in this expanding curriculum.

Made in the USA
Columbia, SC
15 September 2022